The ABRSM SONGBOOK

Book 3

ABRSM

Compiled by Ross Campbell, Robert Forbes and Lilija Zobens

Published by ABRSM (Publishing) Ltd, a wholly owned subsidiary of ABRSM

© 2008 by The Associated Board of the Royal Schools of Music

Reprinted in 2009, 2010, 2012, 2013, 2014

ISBN 978 1 86096 599 9

AB 3130

The publisher has made every effort to contact all copyright owners and owners of print rights to obtain permission for the worldwide use of each work in this book. It requests any rights owners who believe they might have an interest in a copyright work in this book and have not been acknowledged to contact the publisher.

Music origination by Barnes Music Engraving Ltd
Cover and text design by Vermillion
Printed in England by Halstan & Co. Ltd, Amersham, Bucks.

Contents

Singers using these books to prepare for ABRSM graded Singing exams are encouraged to check the current syllabus for full details of requirements before making their choices.

Introduction

The ABRSM Songbook series includes five progressively graded anthologies of song repertoire for teachers and singers of all ages and voice types.

Encompassing a wide range of periods, genres, themes and moods, the series is designed to provide musical interest and technical challenge over many years of vocal study, suggest varied choices for recital programming, and make available selected repertoire for those preparing for ABRSM graded Singing exams. As well as including over 100 art songs of the highest quality (many in new arrangements or editions), the series also contains a truly international collection of 60 unaccompanied traditional songs representing 26 different countries.

Every piece has been expertly researched and is presented here in clear new engraving. Song texts are always given both in their original language and with an English-language singing translation (many of which were specially commissioned for the series). Some of the songs have been transposed from their original keys to ensure that they can be sung by as wide a range of voice types as possible. For all songs, helpful background notes have been included. The collections are topped off with a CD containing 'minus-one' piano recordings of the art song accompaniments, in addition to spoken pronunciation guides for every original text, narrated by native speakers. CD track numbers are given within ⓟ before each piece. We hope that these useful extra features will help singers and teachers with the study and performance of this wealth of wonderful songs.

Biographies

Ross Campbell is Professor of Singing at the Royal Academy of Music, London, and Head of Singing and Music at Guildford School of Acting.

Robert Forbes was formerly Head of Singing at the Birmingham School of Speech and Drama, and is currently Singing Tutor at the Guildford School of Acting.

Lilija Zobens is a singing teacher in Enfield and Hertfordshire schools. She studied folklore with the singer and collector A. L. (Bert) Lloyd and has researched and performed songs of the Balkans and her native Latvia.

Carol Barratt is a composer and leading music educationalist. Her compositions range from works for young children to concert repertoire.

Art Songs

Compiled by Ross Campbell
and Robert Forbes

Compilers' note

It was a rare opportunity and privilege to play, sing through and analyse every song that appears in the ABRSM syllabus for Grade 3. The experience revealed the wide range of song repertoire covered by the syllabus lists. It was therefore not an easy task to select which of the many fine songs should be included in this songbook, so it is important to explain the criteria which affected our choices.

The foremost thought in our minds was how the structure of the exam should inform the early stages of programme planning for a recital; our choices were made in order to present a range of styles and periods, with differing moods and pace, to encourage an interesting and varied exam programme – of the sort that is also expected in a recital. We also considered that the songbook choices should present a variety of technical demands appropriate to the grade, be accessible to all voice types, and be suitable for as wide an age range as possible. Finally, we chose some songs which are not often performed, but which, because of their quality, deserve to be brought before a wider audience.

However, it needs to be said that this songbook is a valuable tool for both teacher and singer irrespective of whether an exam is to be undertaken. By presenting a selection of songs from the folk, classical, musical theatre and light music styles, this songbook should be a benchmark to which the singer can aspire, as well as a rich source of vocal repertoire.

Ross Campbell and Robert Forbes

Notes on the editorial approach

Most public domain works have been re-edited from contemporary sources. Key signatures and time signatures have been modernized. Tempo marks have been supplied where the original has none, also a few additional dynamics; details of research and editorial changes can be found in the 'Notes on the art songs' (pp. 6–10), though obvious errors have been corrected without comment. All metronome marks in square brackets are editorial. Melismatic slurs have been provided for the vocal line without comment, whether or not they occur in the source. Beaming of the vocal part has also been modernized. Where songs have been transposed from the original, the figured bass has been modified to fit the new key. Suggestions for ornamentation have been given above the stave where appropriate, but it is hoped that singers will be encouraged to invent their own.

As far as possible, early published sources have been used for the melodies of folksongs.

I must thank the librarians of the British Library and the Royal College of Music for their help; also Kathleen Bentley for finding sources of the French folksongs, Dr Rhian Davies for checking the texts of the Welsh folksongs, Lada Valesova for help with Czech text, and Jose Luis Rodriguez for information on 'La Cucaracha'.

Michael Pilkington

Notes by (in alphabetical order) Anthony Burton, Ross Campbell and Robert Forbes, with contributions from Michael Pilkington

Notes on the art songs

Ah! how pleasant 'tis to love

Henry Purcell (1659–95) was one of the greatest of all English composers. In his all too short career, he wrote extensively for the church, for the royal court, and for the London theatre. He had a special gift for vocal music: in a posthumous collection of songs, his publisher Henry Playford praised his 'Genius to express the energy of *English* Words, whereby he mov'd the Passions of all his Auditors'. 'Ah! how pleasant 'tis to love' was printed in Purcell's lifetime, in two anthologies both published in 1688. The right hand of the keyboard part here has been supplied by the editor. The song is in quick minuet time: a feeling of one beat to the bar will help you to shape the four-bar phrases.

Sources: *Vinculum Societatis, or The Tie of Good Company*, The Second Book (John Carr and R. C., 1688); *The Banquet of Musick*, The Second Book (Henry Playford, 1688)

Dalmatian Cradle Song

The Scottish musician Sir Hugh (Stevenson) Roberton (1874–1952) was the founding conductor of the Glasgow Orpheus Choir, which made several much-loved recordings, and he composed and arranged many songs for choirs and solo voices. Most of his arrangements are of Scottish songs. But this one, published in 1939, is of a lullaby which he transcribed from a singer in the coastal region of Dalmatia, then part of Yugoslavia and now mostly in Croatia. The song should be sung with a lilt, two beats to the bar. It is in the Dorian mode, the scale running from D to D on the white notes of the keyboard, which is frequently used in Renaissance music and in folksongs in many countries. Singer and pianist should make sure all their Bs and Cs are naturals!

Die Bekehrte

Ignaz Brüll (1846–1907) was born in Moravia in the present-day Czech Republic, but grew up in Vienna, where he achieved success as a pianist and composer even before the age of 20. He was a valued friend of a more famous composer, Johannes Brahms: the two went on walks and holidays together, and tried out Brahms's new orchestral pieces on two pianos. Brüll's own works include several operas, a genre Brahms never attempted, as well as a symphony, concertos, chamber music, piano music and many songs. This song is a setting of a poem by the great German writer Johann Wolfgang von Goethe (1749–1832) which was also set by Hugo Wolf. Damon is a conventional name for a shepherd in depictions of the classical world: here he is represented as playing a haunting tune on his flute which leaves his girlfriend feeling sad. The marking *quasi flauto* in the piano part means 'like a flute', and applies to the melodic phrases in the right hand throughout the song.

Ferry me across the water

Gerald Finzi (1901–56) was one of the leading English composers of his generation, and was especially admired for his sensitive treatment of English words, both for chorus and for solo voice. His first published work, written in 1920/21, was a set of *Ten Children's Songs* to words by the well-known Victorian poet Christina Rossetti (1830–94). These were originally for two-part sopranos and piano, but Finzi later revised this one with a single vocal line. The song is a folk-like dialogue between a girl, represented always in the home minor key, and a ferryman, always in major keys and louder. These distinctions will help singer and pianist to suggest two separate characters. A tempo of ♩= 84 is acceptable for exam purposes.

God be in my head

Sir Henry Walford Davies (1869–1941) sang as a chorister at St George's, Windsor, and studied composition at the Royal College of Music in London. He was organist at the Temple Church in London for 20 years, professor of music at the University of Wales, and Master of the King's Musick from 1934 until his death. He was also well known for his radio broadcasts on music, for schools as well as for adult listeners. Although he composed an oratorio, *Everyman*, and some other large-scale choral works, it is Walford Davies's smaller pieces that are best remembered: the instrumental *Solemn Melody*, several Christmas carols and hymns, and 'God be in my head'. This setting of words from a 16th-century printed Book of Hours, a collection of prayers and other texts for different times of day, was published in 1910 as the first in a collection of short anthems called *Songs for Church and Home*. In the version printed here, the original harmonization is presented in the piano part, while the voice sings the top line. The number of beats to the bar is variable, following the words, and the singer will need to take a breath in his or her own time at each double-bar, before leading the start of the new line.

I'm learning to read
Betty Roe was born in 1930 in London, and worked briefly as a clerk at the Associated Board before going to the Royal Academy of Music to study piano, cello, singing and composition. She has had a long career as church organist and conductor, singer, director of music at the London Academy of Music and Dramatic Art, and composer of church music, songs, and many musicals for schools. *The Banky Field*, with words by John Oliver, was first performed in 1983 by Meole Brace School in Shrewsbury. It is set in an 18th-century mining village on the outskirts of Shrewsbury, and it includes some real-life characters in its fictional story. 'I'm learning to read' is sung by a boy from the local coal mine. It is in fast waltz time, best felt as one-in-a-bar, with several rallentandos and a few bars in verse 3 at a slower speed, but always resuming the original tempo.

In the garden flowers are growing
W. H. (William Henry) Anderson (1882–1955) embarked on a singing career in London, but was forced by chronic bronchitis to seek a drier climate, and in 1910 emigrated to Canada. He settled in Winnipeg, Manitoba, where he became well known as a singing teacher, choral conductor, and composer of songs and choral music. In the words of the *Encyclopedia of Music in Canada*, 'he also arranged a large number of Ukrainian, Czech, and Icelandic folksongs for the Winnipeg choir director Walter Bohonos, using particularly those variants developed among European settlers in Manitoba.' This is one of a pair of Ukrainian songs first published in 1948. The English words are Anderson's own adaptation.

Komm, liebe Zither, komm
The Austrian composer Wolfgang Amadeus Mozart (1756–91) is famous today for his operas, symphonies, concertos, choral works and much else besides; but his songs are a relatively little-known part of his output. This one is the second of two songs with mandolin accompaniment probably written in the winter of 1780/81 in Munich, where Mozart had gone for the rehearsals and first performances of his opera *Idomeneo*. A note on a hand-written copy says that it was written for a Munich horn player named Lang; however, Mozart's original manuscript is lost, and his authorship has been questioned. The anonymous poem is addressed to the zither, a horizontal box-shaped plucked-string instrument. It is represented by the mandolin, also a plucked-string instrument but smaller and more portable; this was used to accompany outdoor serenades, as it is in Mozart's 1787 opera *Don Giovanni*. The mandolin part is shown as the right hand of the piano part; an optional left-hand part has been added by the editor. A piano accompaniment must be used in the exam.
Source: W. A. Mozart: *Gesänge für eine Singstimme mit Klavierbegleitung*, ed. Max Friedlaender (Peters, *c*.1915)

Llwyn Onn
'Llwyn Onn' or 'The Ash Grove' is an old Welsh harp melody, which at different times has been sung to many different lyrics in Welsh and English, including patriotic, comic and satirical songs, hymns, and even a Christmas carol. The tune first appeared in print, without text, in Edward Jones's *The Bardic Museums* in 1802; a few years later it was published in a collection of *Welsh Melodies with Appropriate English Words*. It is given here as it appears in a volume of *Welsh Melodies* published in 1862, edited by John Thomas (1826–1913), harpist to Queen Victoria and Edward VII, with Welsh and English poetry by John Jones ('Talhaiarn', 1810–69) and Thomas Oliphant (1799–1873). The accompaniment is newly composed; Carol Barratt suggests that if it is played on a digital piano the 'harpsichord' voice might be suitable.

Minnelied

Franz Schubert (1797–1828) spent most of his short life in obscurity in Vienna, the capital of the Austro-Hungarian empire, composing operas, orchestral works, chamber and keyboard music, and more than 600 songs including many masterpieces. This 'Minnelied' was written in May 1816 when he was 19. The poem is one of many which he selected from the works of Ludwig Christoph Heinrich Hölty (1748–76); there is a well-known later setting by Brahms. The title 'Minnelied' evokes associations with medieval songs of courtly love addressed to an unattainable and idealized lady. The song moves in a moderate 6/8 time; the acciaccaturas in bb. 13, 15 and 17 should be sung quickly and lightly before the main note. The *sim.* in b. 2 of the piano part is editorial.

Source: F. Schubert: *Gesänge für eine Singstimme mit Klavierbegleitung*, ed. Max Friedlaender (Peters, 1930)

My House

The American Leonard Bernstein (1918–90) was one of the great conductors of his time, and a composer equally successful on the concert platform and in the musical theatre. In 1949 he was asked to write the music for a Broadway production of J. M. Barrie's popular play *Peter Pan*, and responded with far more music than was needed; only in 2005 was the full score issued on disc for the first time. But the songs that were used (with words chiefly by Bernstein himself) contributed to the success of the production, which ran for a year. One of them was 'My House', sung by Wendy after Peter Pan has brought her to Neverland to be mother to his gang of Lost Boys. In her sleep she imagines the kind of house she would like the boys to build for her. The main part of the song should be sung very slowly and smoothly, as if in a dream.

'Orrible Little Blue-Eyes

If 'I'm learning to read' (see above) is for boys, this Betty Roe song is definitely for girls. It comes from the first musical that the composer wrote for schools, *The Barnstormers*, performed in the mid-1970s by Fox Primary School in Notting Hill Gate in west London. The words are by a teacher at the school, Marian Lines (born 1933), who became one of the composer's regular collaborators. The story is about a travelling family theatre group in the 19th century which sets up its shows in barns across the countryside. ''Orrible Little Blue-Eyes' is sung by one of the 'acts'; the last few words of each verse and the coda were originally for chorus, but the words have been adapted for solo singing throughout. The style is that of the music-hall: the singer should 'milk' the pauses at the start of each verse and at the end of verses 1 and 2 (longer each time, perhaps?), and put plenty of energy into the words. The joke of the song (and the challenge to performers) is that the character appears sweet, with her 'big blue eyes', but freely admits that she is really, in Betty Roe's own description, 'very objectionable'.

Sicilian River Song

Maurice Jacobson (1896–1976) was an English composer, pianist and publisher, but also became well known internationally as a festival adjudicator. The *New Grove Dictionary of Music and Musicians* describes him as 'a lively and engaging composer in a variety of genres'; his major work was a large-scale cantata called *The Hound of Heaven*. This adaptation of an 'arietta' or 'little song' from Sicily was published in 1954, originally as a song for unison voices and piano. The marking *alla danza* means 'in dance style'. Notice that the minor-key middle section of each verse has contrasting dynamics and, for the storm in the second verse, a faster tempo.

Sweet and low

Sir Joseph Barnby (1838–96) was a chorister at York Minster, and studied at the Royal Academy of Music in London, before a career as a church organist and choral conductor. In later life he was precentor, effectively director of music, at Eton College, and principal of the Guildhall School of Music and Drama in London. His compositions include hymn tunes and other music for services. But his most famous work is 'Sweet and low', a setting of one of the self-contained 'songs' within the long poem *The Princess* by Alfred, Lord Tennyson (1809–92). It was published as a part-song for mixed choir in 1863, and has often been arranged in close harmony for male or female voices. In this version, the original harmonization is

presented in the piano part, while the voice sings the top line. The song is a lullaby, and should be sung smoothly and gently, with two beats to the bar, and with careful attention to the detailed dynamic markings.
Source: first edition of part-song (London, 1863)

The Banks of Allan Water

'The Banks of Allan Water' is a ballad describing the sad fate of a miller's daughter who lived by the Allan Water, a Scottish river which rises in the Ochil Hills and flows into the Forth near Stirling. It was included in a comic opera performed in London in 1812 called *Rich and Poor*. This had words by the English author M. G. Lewis (1775–1818) – known as 'Monk' Lewis on account of his popular Gothic novel *The Monk* – and music composed and arranged by Charles Edward Horn (1786–1849). However, in Horn's published piano arrangements the song is attributed to 'a Lady' – as it is in an arrangement published in 1828 by Thomas Attwood (1765–1838), Mozart's only English pupil. The latter is the source of the tune as given here, though Attwood's added decorations have been removed, and the piano accompaniment is newly composed.

The Owls

Peter Jenkyns (1921–96) taught in schools in Hertfordshire and later at a college of education across the border in Bedfordshire; he was also a festival adjudicator, singer and musical director. His compositions include a number of tuneful songs for unison singing, which may also be sung as solos. 'The Owls', published in 1961, creates a nocturnal atmosphere with its minor key and its stealthy accompaniment. The phrases become smoother, and the voice could be fuller, at the *meno mosso* sections of each verse; but note that the owls' cries are always very quiet, and need a distinctive colour.

The Path to the Moon

Eric (Harding) Thiman (1900–75), largely self-taught, enjoyed a successful career in London as a teacher, organist and composer, and travelled extensively as an examiner and festival adjudicator. Although he wrote some large-scale choral cantatas and orchestral music, he is best remembered as the composer of vocal and keyboard music suitable for amateurs and schools. 'The Path to the Moon', a setting of a poem by Madeline C. Thomas, was first published in 1956. The piano sets up a gentle two-in-a-bar movement suggesting the lapping of waves, which supports the singer's legato phrases. Notice the cross-rhythms implying 3/4 time in the voice part at the end of each verse, and the graceful melodic curve towards and away from the climax – extending over four bars in the first verse, and stretched to five bars in the second.

The Sunflower

The Irish poet Thomas Moore (1779–1852), a friend of Byron and Shelley, achieved fame through his *Irish Melodies*, a series of volumes published between 1808 and 1834 consisting of newly written English words matched with traditional Irish tunes. Moore's poem 'Believe me, if all those endearing young charms' was set to a melody which had first appeared in print in the mid-18th century, and had previously been known with the alternative text 'My lodging is on the cold ground'. The song is a husband's expression of marital devotion, but it should be sung without excessive sentimentality, in two beats to the bar rather than six: the original tune was a jig.

Wiegenlied

This 'Cradle Song' or lullaby is usually thought to be a German folksong, but in fact its text was written by Stephan Schütze and its music by Wilhelm Taubert (1811–91). Taubert was a childhood friend of Mendelssohn who became director of music at the Berlin court; he published over 200 works, including operas, symphonies and a good deal of piano music, but he was best known for his children's songs. Taubert's melody, here given a new accompaniment, should be sung in long, smooth phrases, and with the subdued dynamics appropriate to a lullaby.

Windy Nights

Irish-born, Sir Charles Villiers Stanford (1852–1924) was one of the first British composers to receive regular performances by orchestras on the European mainland, and had an enormous influence on British music through his teaching at the Royal College of Music in London. His large catalogue of works includes many songs. This one was written in 1892 as part of a cycle of unison songs called *A Child's Garland of Songs*, setting poems from the popular collection *A Child's Garland of Verses* by the Scottish writer Robert Louis Stevenson (1850–94). But Stanford revised it as a solo song in 1914, and that is the version given here. The piano part depicts the galloping of the mysterious night rider (a smuggler?); its *staccato* marking is not meant to apply to the voice. For its full effect the song requires clear articulation of the words and careful attention to dynamics. These differ considerably in the 1892 and 1914 versions: those printed here represent an attempt to provide a consistent version reconciling these variants.

Source: *Windy Nights* (Curwen, 1914)

Disc 1

(1) Piano accompaniment

(2) Pronunciation guide

Original key: C

Ah! how pleasant 'tis to love

Z. 353

Henry Purcell
(1659–95)
ed. Michael Pilkington

[♩ = c.132]

1. Ah! how plea-sant 'tis to love, Ev-'ry mo-ment does im-prove: Joys sur-pris-ing now I meet, Noth-ing's like love so charm-ing sweet.

2. Some do make a god of plea-sure, Oth-ers wor-ship hoard-ed trea-sure; While the lov-er's still ad-dress-ing To his nymph, for ev-'ry bless-ing.

Disc 1

③ Piano accompaniment

④ Pronunciation guide

to Monica Leithley

Dalmatian Cradle Song

P. A. Grand

Tune noted from the singing of
a peasant in Dalmatia

arr. Hugh S. Roberton
(1874–1952)

CHORUS

Hush, my babe, my lit-tle one,___ Thy fa - ther sails the deep;___ But

warm thy bed is, pret-ty one;___ Lie still my dear and sleep.

1. Cold the wind is blow - ing,____ An - gry is the sea;____
2. When the morn shall break a - gain____ O - ver hill and lea;____

Guard, ye saints, his go - ing,____ And bring him back_ to me.____
Then my love shall wake a - gain,____ And dance on dad - dy's knee.____

CHORUS

Hush, my babe, my lit - tle one,____ Thy fa - ther sails the deep;____ But

warm thy bed is, pret - ty one;____ Lie still my dear and sleep. sleep.

Disc 1

⑤ Piano accompaniment

⑥ Pronunciation guide

Die Bekehrte

The Encounter

Johann Wolfgang von Goethe
(1749–1832)

English words by Richard Graves

Ignaz Brüll
(1846–1907)

1. Bei dem Glanz der A - bend - rö - te ging ich still den Wald ent -
   Through the wood-land I was stray-ing, And my heart was filled with
2. Und er zog mich an sich nie - der, küß - te mich so_ hold und
   Then he put his arm a - round me, Said 'It's you that_ I a -

- lang,
pain;
süß.
- *dore!'*

Disc 1

(9) Piano accompaniment

(10) Pronunciation guide

God be in my head

Pynson's *Horae*: A Book of Hours, Sarum 1514

Walford Davies
(1869–1941)
arr. Neil Jenkins from 'Sing Solo Sacred'

Disc 1

⑦ Piano accompaniment

⑧ Pronunciation guide

Ferry me across the water

No. 7 from *Ten Children's Songs*, Op. 1

Christina Rossetti
(1830–94)

Gerald Finzi
(1901–56)

Disc 1

(11) Piano accompaniment

(12) Pronunciation guide

I'm learning to read

from *The Banky Field*

John Oliver

Betty Roe
(born 1930)

rall.   a tempo

be a fine man and stand ten foot tall. I'll ask for your hand, and
buy me some land and I'll plant a tree. I'll ask for your hand, and

when we are wed, I'll buy you a bon-net and gown of
when we are wed, I'll buy you a house and a big brass

red.
bed.

2. I'm
3. I'm

learn-ing to read, I'm learn-ing to write, I'm leav-ing the world that turns

poco a poco cresc.

Disc 1

⑬ Piano accompaniment

⑭ Pronunciation guide

In the garden flowers are growing

No. 2 from *Ukrainian Folk Songs*

Ukrainian traditional

arr. W. H. Anderson

(1882–1955)

1. In the gar-den flow'rs are grow-ing, Tom-ta drit-ta, tom-ta dra!
2. Boys! to quar-rel, is so cra-zy,

Boys will quar-rel where I'm go-ing, Tom-ta drit-ta, tom-ta dra! Hoy, hoy, hoy-a, hoy-a!
Pret-ty girls are al-ways la-zy,

How my lit-tle head is ach-ing; Hoy, hoy, hoy-a, hoy-a! Oh! the trou-ble I am mak-ing!

Disc 1

(15) Piano accompaniment

(16) Pronunciation guide

Komm, liebe Zither, komm

Come sweetest zither, come

K. 351

English words by
Elizabeth Eva Leach

Wolfgang Amadeus Mozart
(1756–91)
ed. Michael Pilkington

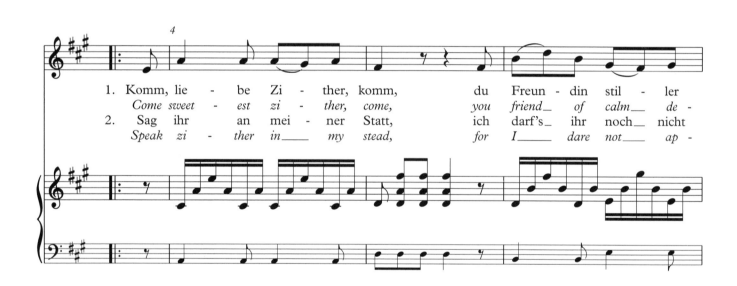

1. Komm, lie - be Zi - ther, komm, du Freun - din stil - ler
   Come sweet - est zi - ther, come, you friend of calm de -
2. Sag ihr an mei - ner Statt, ich darf's ihr noch nicht
   Speak zi - ther in my stead, for I dare not ap -

Lie - be, du sollst auch mei - ne Freun - din sein.
- vo - tion, I would thy friend - ship now at - tain.
sa - gen, wie ihr so ganz mein Herz ge - hört;
- proach her, She who has all my trem - bling heart.

Disc 1

(17) Piano accompaniment

(18) Pronunciation guide

Llwyn Onn

The Ash Grove

John Jones
(1810–69)

English words by
Thomas Oliphant (1799–1873)

Welsh traditional

arr. Carol Barratt

Disc 1

21 Piano accompaniment

22 Pronunciation guide

My House

from *Peter Pan*

Words and music by
Leonard Bernstein
(1918–90)

AB 3130

Disc 1

(19) Piano accompaniment

(20) Pronunciation guide

Original key: E

Minnelied

Love-song

D. 429

Ludwig Christoph Heinrich Hölty
(1748–76)

English words by
Elizabeth Eva Leach

Franz Schubert
(1797–1828)

ed. Michael Pilkington

9

Rö - ter blü - hen Tal__ und Au, grü - ner wird der Ra - sen,
All the blooms do red - der seem, Green - er grows the lawn__ there,
Trau - te, min - nig - li - che Frau, wol - lest nim - mer flie - hen;
Oh, my sweet, my la - dy good, Look to leave me ne - ver;

13

wo mir Blu - men rot und blau ih - re Hän - de la - sen,
Where she picks flow'rs by the stream, By her I am drawn__ there,
daß mein Herz, gleich die - ser Au, mög' in Won - ne blü - hen,
So my heart like this fair wood, Might bloom hap - py ev - er,

17

wo mir Blu - men rot und blau ih - re Hän - de la - sen.
Where she picks flow'rs by the stream, By her I__ am drawn__ there.
daß mein Herz, gleich die - ser Au, mög' in Won - ne blü - hen.
So my heart like this fair wood, Might bloom hap - py ev - er!

21

Disc 1

(23) Piano accompaniment
(24) Pronunciation guide

'Orrible Little Blue-Eyes

from *The Barnstormers*

Marian Lines
(born 1933)

Betty Roe
(born 1930)

loved ones all say 'drop it', I'm a sto - ry - tell - ing mop - pet, With my
sure don't come much glib - ber Than this ta - lent - ed 'ad - lib - ber' With her
tri - ple tre - ble trou - ble, Still I can't re - sist a bub - ble While I

1. 2.
big blue eyes! With my big blue eyes! With my big blue eyes!
eyes of blue! With her eyes of blue!

3.
flut - ter at the dou - ble With my great big eyes of blue! With my

great big eyes of bloooooooooo!

Disc 1

25 Piano accompaniment

26 Pronunciation guide

Sicilian River Song

Margaret A. Jack

From a manuscript of Sicilian ariettas

arr. Maurice Jacobson
(1896–1976)

Disc 1

27 Piano accompaniment

28 Pronunciation guide

Sweet and low

Alfred, Lord Tennyson
(1809–92)

Joseph Barnby
(1838–96)

ed. Michael Pilkington

Sweet and low, sweet and low, Wind of the west-ern sea,___ Low, low,

breathe and blow, Wind of the west-ern sea!___ O-ver the roll-ing wa-ters go,

Come from the dy-ing moon, and blow, Blow him a-gain to me;___ While my lit-tle one,

Disc 1
29 Piano accompaniment
30 Pronunciation guide

The Banks of Allan Water

M. G. Lewis
(1775–1818)

Melody 'by a Lady'
arr. Carol Barratt

1. On the banks of Al - lan Wa - ter, When the
   banks of Al - lan Wa - ter, When brown
   banks of Al - lan Wa - ter, When the

sweet spring - time did_ fall____ Was the Mill - er's love - ly
Au - tumn spreads its__ store,___ There I saw the Mill - er's
win - ter snow fell_ fast,____ Still was seen the Mill - er's

daugh - ter, Fair - est of them all. For his
daugh - ter, But she smiled no more. For the
daugh - ter, Chill - ing blew the blast. But the

bride_____ a sol - dier sought her, And a win - ning tongue had
sum - mer grief had brought her, And the sol - dier false was
Mill - er's love - ly daugh - ter, Both from cold and care was

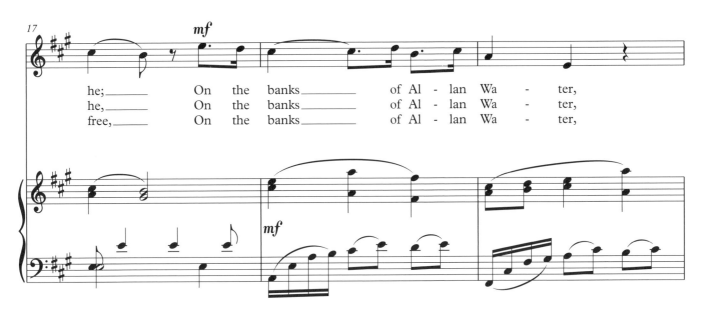

he;_____ On the banks_____ of Al - lan Wa - ter,
he,_____ On the banks_____ of Al - lan Wa - ter,
free,_____ On the banks_____ of Al - lan Wa - ter,

last time, to Coda ⊕

None was gay as she.
None was sad as she.
There a corpse lay

2. On the
3. On the

⊕ **CODA**

molto rit.

she.

Disc 1

(33) Piano accompaniment

(34) Pronunciation guide

The Path to the Moon

Madeline C. Thomas

Eric H. Thiman
(1900–75)

Sil - ver the sails to car - ry me, to car - ry, car - ry,

car - ry me o - ver the sea.

So will I sail, on a star - ry night On the

path to the Moon, a sea - bird's flight; Skim-ming the waves, where the fish - es play,

Tra - vel-ling on, for ma - ny a day;

Sil - ver the sails to car - ry me, to

car - ry, car - ry, car - ry me o - ver the

sea.

Disc 1

(31) Piano accompaniment

(32) Pronunciation guide

for Leila Tyrrill and the Oakwood Choir

The Owls

Words and music by
Peter Jenkyns
(1921–96)

Disc 1
(35) Piano accompaniment
(36) Pronunciation guide

The Sunflower

Thomas Moore
(1779–1852)

Irish traditional
arr. Carol Barratt

It__ is not while beau - ty and youth are thine own, And thy cheeks un-pro-faned by a tear,_____ That the fer - vour and faith of a soul can be known, To which time will but make thee more dear!_____ Oh! the heart, that has tru - ly loved, ne - ver for-gets, But as

tru - ly loves on to the close;_____ As the sun - flow-er turns to her

god, when he sets, The same look which she turned when he

rose!_____

Disc 1

(37) Piano accompaniment

(38) Pronunciation guide

Original key: D

Wiegenlied

Cradle Song

Op. 27 No. 5

Stephan Schütze

English words by
Elizabeth Eva Leach

Wilhelm Taubert
(1811–91)

arr. Carol Barratt

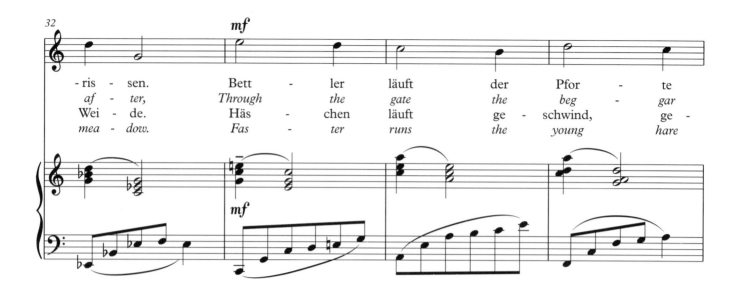

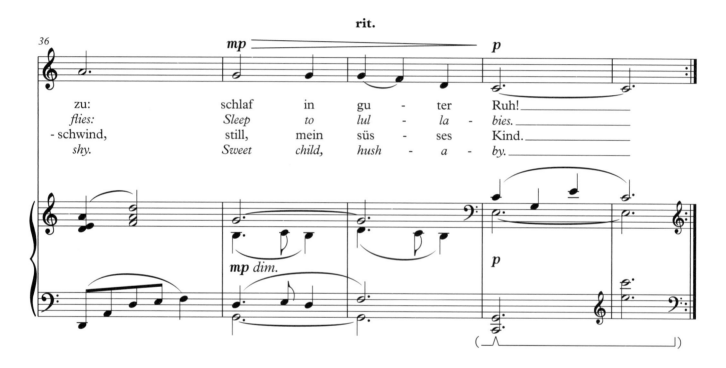

3. Schlaf die Wänglein rot,
   hast noch keine Not,
   Täubchen fliegt auf Feld und Flur,
   fliegt und sucht ein Körnchen nur.
   Ach die Kleinen, still und bange,
   sprechen: 'Mutter bleibt so lange.'
   Mutter bleibt bis Abendrot,
   schlaf, hast keine Not!

4. Kannst nur ruhig sein,
   Bettler kehrt schon ein,
   Häschen schläft auf Stacheldorn,
   Häschen liegt nun schon im Korn,
   Täubchen füttert seine Jungen,
   Vöglein hat nun ausgesungen,
   müd' ist alles gross und klein,
   schlaf nun ruhig ein.

3. *Rosy-cheeked you yawn,*
   Pampered you were born.
   Birdie flies through gathered wheat
   Searching for one grain to eat.
   Ah, her chicks chirp this sad songlet:
   'Why has mummy not come back yet?'
   Their mum's gone from dusk to dawn –
   Pampered you were born!

4. *Sleep, my sugarplum:*
   Back the beggar's come,
   And the lev'ret sleeps again,
   In the hedge out of the rain.
   Birdie feeds her chicks with barley,
   Singing in the morning early.
   Great and small have had their crumb.
   Sleep, my sugarplum.

Disc 1

39 Piano accompaniment

40 Pronunciation guide

Windy Nights

Robert Louis Stevenson
(1850–94)

Charles Villiers Stanford
(1852–1924)
ed. Michael Pilkington

Traditional Songs

Compiled by Lilija Zobens
and Leslie East

Compilers' note

One of the distinctive features of the ABRSM Singing syllabus is the requirement for candidates to offer an unaccompanied traditional song of their own choice. Full details are given in the syllabus booklet.

In *The ABRSM Songbook* series we have collected together some traditional songs suitable for this part of the Singing exam. Our collection has ranged widely, encompassing 26 countries. Our aim has been to extend the horizons of teachers and candidates, to take in songs from a variety of traditions, and to reflect in some part the origins of ABRSM examinees. We believe that candidates will enjoy the challenge of presenting a song from their own culture or, indeed, a song that comes from someone else's.

We have presented these songs here in a straightforward way. The main philosophy has been to encourage the singing of them in their original form and language. Then it has been the intention to tempt the singer into exploring and understanding the song from his or her own perspective. Explanations are given where thought necessary. Songs in English are in some cases accompanied by a brief explanation as to the song's meaning or origin where the words themselves are not explicit. Songs in other languages are given with their original language first and an English-singing version underneath or alongside. Either language could be used in an exam. In the case of Chinese and Greek songs, a transliteration of the original text is provided and the text is also given in the characters of the language. On the accompanying CD, each song can be heard pronounced in the original language. Even the English-language texts have been recorded, where possible in an appropriate accent.

When preparing one of these songs, it is important to experiment with the pitch to be used. Many traditional songs have extraordinarily wide ranges or very high or very low tessituras. Many in this collection have been notated at the pitch level used by the singer from whom the song was originally collected and recorded. Traditional singers always try to find a pitch level for a song that suits their own voices and singers using this collection should do the same.

Another area of freedom is in the interpretation of speed, dynamics and expression. Our collection gives only very brief guidance in this area or omits any guidance at all as traditional singers would be expected to develop their own distinctive interpretation of a song. The student should be encouraged to determine the way in which each of these songs might be sung through an understanding of the words, the meaning of the song and the musical character of the tune. Some songs have been notated with distinctive ornamentation but this shows merely a 'snapshot' of the song in one interpretation and candidates could ignore some or all of the ornamentation shown.

If one of these songs is chosen to be sung in an exam, then the student should ensure that its duration complies with the syllabus regulation shown. It is perfectly reasonable with traditional songs to make a selection of verses that make sense together, rather than sing the complete song.

Finally, it should be noted that the traditional songs gathered together here are NOT songs prescribed for ABRSM exams though obviously we hope they will be used for that purpose! They are intended as a resource for teachers and their students, to provide repertoire and an *approximate* guide to the standard of difficulty that might be appropriate to each grade. Sources of other traditional songs should be explored by teacher and student, especially songs from the student's own culture, or songs that show off a student's facility with another language. ABRSM examiners will welcome a rich variety of traditional songs when they examine singers in countries around the world.

Lilija Zobens and Leslie East

The collection of traditional songs was compiled by Lilija Zobens, with the assistance of Professor Jonathan Stock of Sheffield University. We are very grateful to Professor Stock for his contribution of songs from Malay, Chinese and Indonesian traditions to these anthologies. Notes on the origins and performance of the songs are by Lilija Zobens and Leslie East.

Disc 2

1 Pronunciation guide

Aa Ola, Ola, min eigen onge!

O Ola, Ola, you did betray me

Norway

1. Aa O - la, O - la, min ei - gen on - ge! Kvi la du
O O - la, O - la, you did be - tray me, And so un -

2. Og mang ei taar paa mi kinn ha run - ne, Eg tenk - te
My mind to you, love, is ev - er turn - ing, My heart for

3. Den dag kjem al - dri, at eg deg gløy - mer, For um eg
When I am dream - ing, when I am wak - ing, My heart for

paa meg den sorg saa tun - ge? Eg tenk - te al - dri, du brydd' deg um, Aa nar - re
- kind - ly, you did for - sake me. On me you've laid hea - vy grief and care; The pain is

ve - te de ha - de sprun - ge, Og eg ha graa - te saa mang ei taar, Som der æ'
you, love, is ev - er burn - ing. For you I've let fall as ma - ny tears As there are

sø - ver, eg um deg drøy - mer. Um natt og dag er du li - ke nær, Og best eg
you, love, is ev - er ach - ing. I feel you near me both day and night, But see you

meg, som du saag va ung, aa nar - re meg, som du saag va ung.
great - er than I can bear, the pain is great - er than I can bear.

da - gar i tu - sen aar, som der æ' da - gar i tu - sen aar.
days in a thou - sand years, as there are days in a thou - sand years.

ser deg, naar myrkt det er, og best eg ser deg, naar myrkt det er.
best in the dim twi - light, but see you best in the dim twi - light.

Do not sing this too fast. It is a very expressive song about loving and longing. Take care to mark the difference between G sharps and G naturals.

Disc 2

(2) Pronunciation guide

A la nanita nana

Hush pretty baby hush

Spain

This beautiful, simple lullaby needs to be sung with warmth and clear articulation. Make the most of the contrast of the major key in the middle line with a brighter tone – but not too bright or you will wake the baby up!

Disc 2

3 Pronunciation guide

All things are quite silent

Sussex, England

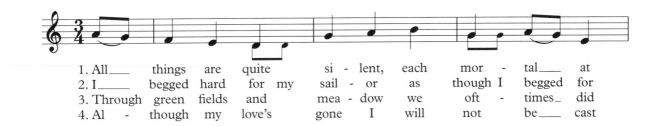

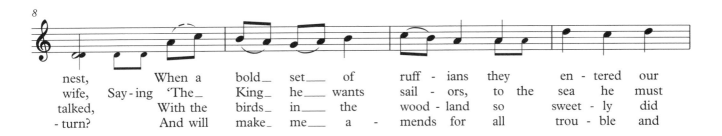

1. All___ things are quite si - lent, each mor - tal___ at rest, When___ me and my love___ got snug in___ one nest, When a bold___ set___ of ruff - ians they en - tered our cave, And they forced my dear jew - el to plough the___ salt wave.

2. I___ begged hard for my sail - or as though I begged for life. They'd not lis - ten to me al - though a___ fond wife, Say-ing 'The___ King___ he___ wants sail - ors, to the sea he must go', And they've left me la - ment - ing in sor - row___ and woe.

3. Through green fields and mea - dow we oft - times___ did walk, And___ sweet con - ver - sa - tion of love we___ have talked, With the birds___ in___ the wood - land so sweet - ly did sing, And the love - ly thrush - es' voi - ces made the val - leys___ to ring.

4. Al - though my love's gone I will not be___ cast down, Who___ knows but my sail - or may once more___ re - turn? And will make___ me___ a - mends for all trou - ble and strife, And my true - love and I might live hap - py___ for life.

This song was notated by Vaughan Williams in Lower Beeding, Sussex, in 1904, but its subject matter obviously refers to the press-gangs which (before around 1835) terrorized coastal areas, forcing men to serve in the Navy.

Disc 2

(4) Pronunciation guide

Coasts of Barbary

Devon, England

1. There were two ships from Eng - land did sail,
2. There is noth-ing a - head, sir, there is noth - ing a - stern, *Blow*
3. Then hail her, hail her! our no - ble cap - tain cried,
4. I am no man of war, no pi - ra - teer to - day,

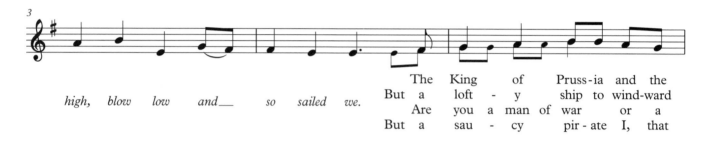

high,   blow   low   and___   so   sailed   we.
The King of Pruss-ia and the
But a loft - y ship to wind-ward
Are you a man of war or a
But a sau - cy pir - ate I, that

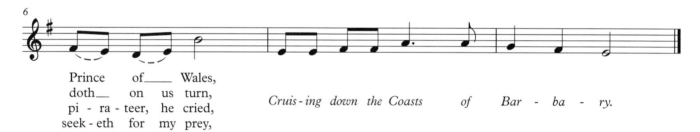

Prince of___ Wales,
doth___ on us turn,
pi - ra - teer, he cried,
seek - eth for my prey,

Cruis - ing   down   the   Coasts   of   Bar - ba - ry.

5. Then ' broadside to broadside, these gallant vessels go,
   Blow high,...

Away the ' English the saucy pirates mast did blow.
   Cruising down...

6. For ' mercy! for mercy! the daring rascals cried,
   Blow high,...
   But the ' mercy we showed them was to sink them in the tide.
   Cruising down...

7. With ' cutlass or gun, they fought for hours three,
   Blow high,...
   The ' ship it was their coffin, their grave it was the sea.
   Cruising down...

You will need to take care over making the text fit the melody. In verses 5–7, the syllables before the ' go on the up-beat.

Disc 2
(5) Pronunciation guide

Cuckoo

Devon, England

1. The__ cuck - oo is a pret - ty bird, she__ sings__ as__ she__
2. O__ meet - ing is a plea - sure but__ part - ing__ is__
3. The__ grave will re - ceive me and__ bring__ me__ to__
4. Come all you fair__ maid - ens wher - ev - er__ you__

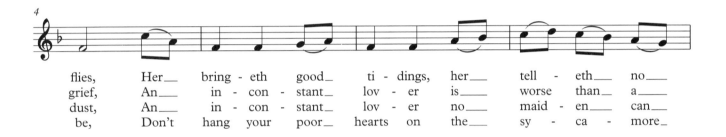

flies, Her__ bring - eth good__ ti - dings, her__ tell - eth__ no__
grief, An__ in - con - stant__ lov - er is__ worse than__ a__
dust, An__ in - con - stant__ lov - er no__ maid - en__ can__
be, Don't hang your poor__ hearts on the__ sy - ca - more__

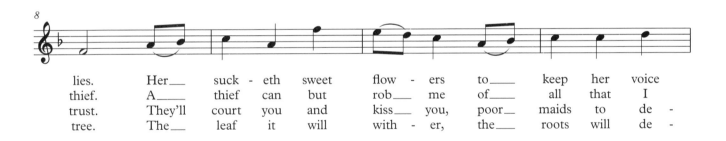

lies. Her__ suck - eth sweet flow - ers to__ keep her voice
thief. A__ thief can but rob__ me of__ all that I
trust. They'll court you and kiss__ you, poor__ maids to de -
tree. The__ leaf it will with - er, the__ roots will de -

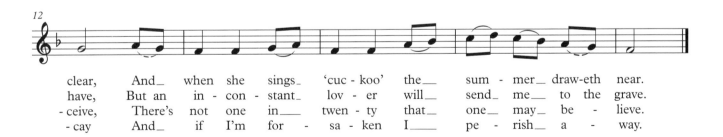

clear, And__ when she sings__ 'cuc - koo' the__ sum - mer__ draw-eth near.
have, But an in - con - stant__ lov - er will__ send__ me__ to the grave.
- ceive, There's not one in__ twen - ty that__ one__ may__ be - lieve.
- cay And__ if I'm for - sa - ken I__ pe - rish__ a - way.

You will need to take care over the speed of this one: too fast, and the sad words will not sound convincing; too slow, and the tune may become too mournful and heavy.

Disc 2

(6) Pronunciation guide

凤阳花鼓
Fengyang huagu 1 and 2

Fengyang Song

Anhui Province, China

Huagu are humorous songs sung by beggars, who accompany themselves with gong and drum rhythms.

Sing these briskly, remembering that they would usually be sung as the performers walked up and down. Sing both, making the character of each distinct.

Disc 2

7 Pronunciation guide

Disc 2
(8) Pronunciation guide

Green Besoms

Devon, England

1. I am a bes-om_ ma-ker, Come list-en to my song, With a bun-dle of green
2. One day as I was trudg-ing Down by my na-tive cot, I saw a jol-ly

bes-oms I trudge the world a-long, Sweet plea-sures that I do en-joy Both morn-ing, night and
farm-er, O hap-py is his lot. He ploughs his fur-rows deep,___ The seed he lay-eth

noon, As I walk o'er the hills so high A-ga-ther-ing of green broom.
low, And there it bides a-sleep Un-til the green broom blow.

O, come and buy my bes-oms,

Bon-ny green broom bes-oms, Bes-oms fine and new, Bon-ny green broom bes-oms Bet-ter nev-er grew.

3. One day as I was walking,
    'Twas down in yonder vale,
I met Jack Spratt the miller
    That taketh toll and tale.
His mill, O how it rattles,
    The grist it grindeth clean.
I ease him of his jingling
    By selling besoms green.
    O, come and buy…

4. One day as I was walking
    Across the hills so high
I saw the wealthy squire,
    Who hath a rolling eye.
I sing my song, he tips a wink,
    And glad the squire did seem.
I ease him of his jingling chink
    By selling besoms green.
    O, come and buy…

5. One day as I was walking
    Along the King's high-way
I met the parson riding
    And ventured him to stay.
The parish tithe that is your due
    Collecting you have been,
But tithe I'll also take of you
    By selling besoms green.
    O, come and buy…

6. O when the yellow broom is ripe
    Upon its native soil,
It's like a pretty baby bright
    With sweet and wavily smile.
My cuts that make the besom
    I bundle tight and spare
All honest folks to please 'em
    I'm the darling of the fair.
    O, come and buy…

A besom is a broom made from a bunch of twigs, and broom is a shrub from which besoms were often made – and surprisingly efficient! A cot is a cottage or small dwelling; grist is corn for grinding; jingling chink is money; and the parish tithe was a tenth of the produce of the land and animals, given to the church.

In verses 3–6 you will have to adjust the rhythm slightly in places, to make the words fit the melody.

Disc 2
(9) Pronunciation guide

Kalevalainen runosävelmä

Lines from the Kalevala

Finland

1. Mie - le - ni mi - nun te - ke - vi, ai - vo - ni a - jat - te - le - vi
   I am driv - en by my long - ing, And my un - der-stand-ing ur - ges
2. Ve - li kul - ta, veik - ko - se - ni, kau - nis kas - vin-kump-pa - li - ni!
   Dear - est friend, and much loved bro - ther, Best be - loved of all com-pan - ions,

läh - te - ä - ni lau - la - ma - han, saa' - a - ni sa - ne - le - ma - han.
That I should com-mence my sing - ing, And be - gin my re - ci - ta - tion.
Lähe nyt kans - sa lau - la - ma - han, saa ke - ra sa - ne - le - ma - han.
Come and let us sing to - ge - ther, Let us now be - gin our con - verse.

Sa - nat suus - sa - ni su - la - vat, pu - he' et pu - to - e - le - vat,
To my mouth the words are flow - ing, And the words are gent - ly fall - ing,
Har - voin yh - te - hen y - hym - me, saam - me toi - nen toi - si - him - me,
Rare - ly can we meet to - ge - ther, Rare - ly one can meet the oth - er,

kie - lel - le - ni ker - ki - ä - vät, ham - pa - hil - le - ni ha - joo - vat.
Quick - ly as my tongue can shape them, And be - tween my teeth e - mer - ging.
näil - lä rau - koil - la ra - joil - la, po - loi - sil - la Poh - jan mail - la.
In these dis - mal North - ern re - gions, In the drear - y land of Poh - ja.

These are the opening lines of the Kalevala, the national epic of Finland, which has been part of the oral tradition among Finnish-speaking people for over two thousand years. The poetry (in the characteristic trochaic tetrameter) was often sung to the accompaniment of the *kantele*, a five-string zither.

Disc 2
(10) Pronunciation guide

Román Castillo

Mexico

1. ¿Dón-de vas, Ro-mán Cas-ti-llo,_ dón-de vas? ¡Po-bre de ti!____ ¿Dón-de
Which way now, Ro-man Cas-ti-llo? Which way now, un-hap-py man!_ Which way

2. An-te-no-che_me di-je-ron_ que pa-sas-te por a-quí,____ An-te-
And last night, so_ I am told, you came and brought your trou-ble here,_ And last

3. ¡Ten pie-dad, Ro-mán Cas-ti-llo,_ ten pie-dad! ¡Po-bre de ti!____ ¡Ten pie-
Have a care, Ro-man Cas-ti-llo, Have a care, un-hap-py man,_ Have a

ti!_____ Ya no bus-ques más que-re-llas_ por nues-tras da-mas de_a-quí.___ Ya no
man!___ Are you proud of_ your ad-ven-tures With the la-dies of this land?___ Are you

-quí,____ Que to-cas-te_ sie-te ve-ces_ y_el can-cel que-rías a-brir.___ Que to-
here.___ Rang the bell thir-teen_ times then_ near-ly broke down my oak door.___ Rang the

ti!____ Si per-sis-tes_ en tu vi-da_ de do-lor voy a mo-rir.____ Si per-
man.___ If you keep on_ mis-be-hav-ing I will die of bit-ter shame,_ If you

-quí.____ Ya_es-tá he-ri-do_ tu ca-ba-llo, ya_es-tá ro-to_ tu_es-pa-
land?____ Now your horse is_ sore-ly wound-ed_ And your sword bro-ken in

-brir.____ Que mis cria-dos_ es-pan-ta-dos_ a na-die que-rían a-
door.____ My poor ser-vant_ you did tor-ment,_ He re-fused to_ turn the

-rir.____ Tú_e-res nob-le,_ tú_e-res bra-vo,_ hom-bre de gran_ co-ra-
shame.____ You are no-ble,_ you're cou-ra-geous_ And your heart is_ made of

-dín,____ Tus ha-za-ñas_ son ex-tra-ñas_ y tu_a-mor no tie-ne fin.____
two,____ Seems this ne-ver-end-ing plea-sure You will seek all your life through._

-brir.____ Y que_en-ton-ces_ tú gri-tas-te:_ ¡A-bran o van a mo-rir!____
key,____ So you rant-ed_ then you shout-ed:_ 'Let me in or I will draw.'____

-zón,____ ¡Pe-ro que tu_a-mor no man-che_ nun-ca mi re-pu-ta-ción!____
gold____ But don't ev-er_ let your lov-ing_ Stain my ho-nour or my name.____

This Mexican version of an ancient ballad or Romance originated in Salamanca in Spain. It is best sung with a two-in-a-bar feeling to reflect the fear and anger of the text.

Disc 2
(11) Pronunciation guide

Seventeen Come Sunday

Sussex, England

1. 'Where are you go-ing, my pret-ty fair maid, Come tell to me, my hon-ey.' The

an-swer that she gave to me, 'On an er-rand for my Mum-my.' *With a*

ru-tum, tu-tum, fol-ly tid-dle-u-tum Ri-fol tid-dle did-dle-i-do.

2. 'How old are you, my pretty fair maid,
   Come tell to me, my honey.'
   The answer that she gave to me,
   'I'm seventeen come Sunday.'
      With a rutum,…

3. 'Can you love me, my pretty fair maid,
   Come tell to me, my honey.'
   The answer that she gave to me,
   'I dare not for my Mummy.'
      With a rutum,…

4. I went down to her Mummy's house,
   The moon was shining clearly;
   I sang beneath her window pane,
   'Your soldier loves you dearly.'
      With a rutum,…

5. 'O, soldier, will you marry me,
   For now's your time or never;
   For if you do not marry me,
   My heart is broke forever.'
      With a rutum,…

6. And now she is the soldier's wife,
   And sails across the brine-O;
   'The drum and fife is my delight,
   And merry man is mine-O.'
      With a rutum,…

This jaunty tune is known in many parts of the English-speaking world. Sing it with energy, with strong articulation of the nonsense syllables in the Chorus, and characterize the quoted passages, perhaps in different types of voice or with contrasting weight of tone.

Disc 2

(12) Pronunciation guide

Stole mi se oženi

Stojan's Wife

Serbia

1. Sto - le mi se o - že - ni, Sto - le mi se o - že - ni,
Sto - jan, for to share his life, Sto - jan, for to share his life,

Sto - le mi se o - že - ni, u - ze že - na ra - bot - na:_____
Sto - jan, for to share his life, Chose a good hard - work - ing wife._____

2. Leb ne znaje da mesi,
   A leb znaje da jede.

3. Stole mi se oženi,
   Uze žena rabotna:

4. Dom ne znaje da mete,
   Doma znaje da sedi!

5. Stole mi se oženi,
   Uze žena rabotna:

6. Mleko ne zna da vari,
   Mleko znaje da jede.

2. *Kneading bread, she could not do,*
   Eating it – now that she knew!

3. *Stojan, for to share his life,*
   Chose a good hard-working wife.

4. *Housework pleased her not a bit,*
   But at home she liked to sit.

5. *Stojan, for to share his life,*
   Chose a good hard-working wife.

6. *Why should she of cooking think,*
   When the milk was there to drink?

A humorous dance-song from Serbia, though this version was collected in Macedonia (now known as FYROM); Stole is simply a pet name for Stojan. Make this bounce, and feel the metre as a fast 2 + 2 + 3, ('allegro giocoso').

English singing translation by E.V. de Bray

Disc 2
(13) Pronunciation guide

Sweet Nightingale

Cornwall, England

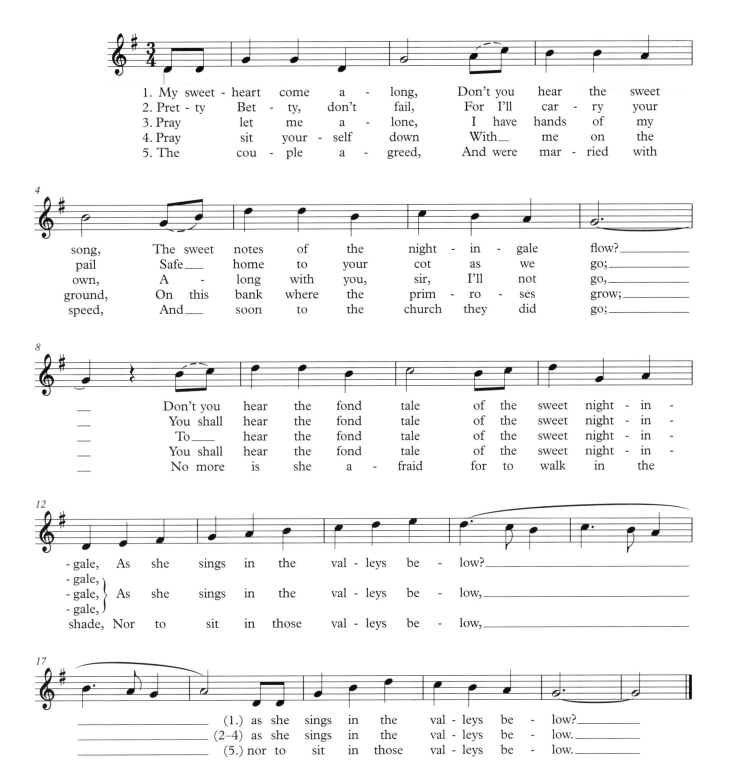

1. My sweet - heart come a - long, Don't you hear the sweet
2. Pret - ty Bet - ty, don't fail, For I'll car - ry your
3. Pray let me a - lone, I have hands of my
4. Pray sit your - self down With__ me on the
5. The cou - ple a - greed, And were mar - ried with

song, The sweet notes of the night - in - gale flow?_____
pail Safe__ home to your cot as we go;_____
own, A - long with you, sir, I'll not go,_____
ground, On this bank where the prim - ro - ses grow;_____
speed, And__ soon to the church they did go;_____

__ Don't you hear the fond tale of the sweet night - in -
__ You shall hear the fond tale of the sweet night - in -
__ To__ hear the fond tale of the sweet night - in -
__ You shall hear the fond tale of the sweet night - in -
__ No more is she a - fraid for to walk in the

- gale, As she sings in the val - leys be - low?_____
- gale,
- gale, } As she sings in the val - leys be - low,_____
- gale,
shade, Nor to sit in those val - leys be - low,_____

_____ (1.) as she sings in the val - leys be - low?_____
_____ (2–4) as she sings in the val - leys be - low._____
_____ (5.) nor to sit in those val - leys be - low._____

This song was first noted from the singing of four Cornish miners in 1854. Keep it flowing, and not too sentimental.